BRIGHT
IDEA
BOOKS

AREA 51

by Aubrey Zalewski

CAPSTONE PRESS
a capstone imprint

T0050799

Bright Idea Books are published by Capstone Press
1710 Roe Crest Drive, North Mankato, Minnesota 56003
www.mycapstone.com

Copyright © 2020 by Capstone Press, a Capstone imprint. All rights reserved. No part of this
publication may be reproduced in whole or in part, or stored in a retrieval system, or transmitted
in any form or by any means, electronic, mechanical, photocopying, recording, or otherwise,
without written permission of the publisher.

Library of Congress Cataloging-in-Publication Data
Names: Zalewski, Aubrey, author.
Title: Area 51 / by Aubrey Zalewski.
Description: North Mankato, Minnesota : Capstone Press, [2020] | Series:
   Aliens | Includes index. | Audience: Grades 4 to 6.
Identifiers: LCCN 2018060998 (print) | LCCN 2019000319 (ebook) | ISBN
   9781543571141 (ebook) | ISBN 9781543571066 (hardcover) | ISBN 9781543574937 (pbk.)
Subjects: LCSH: Unidentified flying objects--Sightings and
   encounters--Nevada--Rachel Region--Juvenile literature. | Extraterrestrial
   beings--Juvenile literature. | Area 51 (Nev.)--Juvenile literature.
Classification: LCC TL789.5.N3 (ebook) | LCC TL789.5.N3 Z35 2020 (print) |
   DDC 358.4/170979314--dc23
LC record available at https://lccn.loc.gov/2018060998

All internet sites appearing in back matter were available and accurate when this book was sent
to press.

Editorial Credits
Editor: Claire Vanden Branden
Designer: Becky Daum
Production Specialist: Melissa Martin

Photo Credits
Alamy: Everett Collection Historical, 22–23, World History Archive, 8–9; iStockphoto: alexeys,
19, Lpettet, 26–27, numbeos, 30–31, powerofforever, 11, 28; NASA: JSC, 16–17; Newscom:
CSU Archives/Everett Collection, 24; Shutterstock Images: Alizada Studios, 6–7, Chromatika
Multimedia snc, cover (UFOs), Leo Blanchette, 14, Nebs, cover (background), Peter Barrett, 20–21,
Sipaphoto, cover (sign), 5, tsuneomp, 12–13

Design Elements: Shutterstock Images, Red Line Editorial

Printed in the United States of America.
PA70

TABLE OF CONTENTS

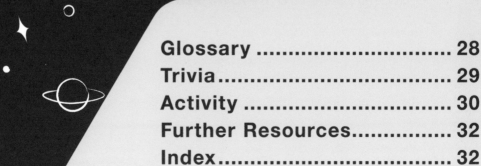

CHAPTER 1

TOP
Secret

Red posts stick up from the ground. Signs tell people to keep out. Guards patrol the area. They make sure people do not get too close. This is Area 51.

WARNING

Restricted Area

It is unlawful to enter this area without permission of the Installation Commander.
Sec. 21, Internal Security Act of 1950; 50 U.S.C. 797

While on this installation all personnel and the property under their control are subject to search.

Use of deadly force authorized.

WARNING!

NO TRESPASSING
AUTHORITY N.R.S. 207-200
MAXIMUM PUNISHMENT: $1000 FINE
SIX MONTHS IMPRISOMENT
OR BOTH
STRICTLY ENFORCED

PHOTOGRAPHY
OF THIS AREA
IS PROHIBITED
18-__-795

WARNING

MILITARY INSTALLATION

IT IS UNLAWFUL TO ENTER THIS INSTALLATION WITHOUT
THE WRITTEN PERMISSION OF THE INSTALLATION COMMANDER.

INSTALLATION COMMANDER
AUTHORITY: Internal Security Act, 50
U.S.C. 797
PUNISHMENT: Up to one year imprisonment
and $5,000. fine.

Signs tell people of Area 51's rules.

Area 51 is a U.S. Air Force base in Nevada. But few people know what goes on there. Only workers are let inside. Even flying above Area 51 is not allowed.

Area 51 is located in a desert.

An image taken from space shows Area 51.

ANOTHER NAME

Area 51 used to be called Paradise Ranch. This was so people would want to work there.

THE BEGINNING

The government built Area 51. It was used during World War II (1939–1945). It was a gun range for fighter airplanes. Then it was not used after the war.

The Central Intelligence Agency (CIA) took over the base in 1955. Soon many CIA workers came to Area 51. Everything was kept top secret.

CHAPTER 2

STRANGE Sightings

Soon people began to see strange things. They saw glowing objects near Area 51. They called them **UFOs**.

The objects moved in odd ways. Some people said they looked like spaceships. People started to believe the objects were from **aliens**.

People started
to tell stories of
seeing UFOs flying
over Area 51.

Some people believe that many alien spaceships have crashed on Earth. They say the government keeps it a secret.

BOB LAZAR'S STORY

One man said he knew the truth. His name was Bob Lazar. Lazar talked to news reporters. He said he worked at Area 51. His work was top secret. He worked in an area called S-4. He said S-4 hid crashed spaceships.

The S-4 workers did tests. They tried to find out how the spaceships worked. Some workers flew them. The spaceships moved in odd ways. They also glowed. That is what people saw flying in the sky.

Many people
started to believe
the government
was hiding aliens
after Lazar's story.

14

Lazar said S-4 had more than just spaceships. It also had dead aliens. He said he saw a photo of one. It was gray. It was less than 4 feet (1.2 meters) tall. He said living aliens had visited Area 51 too. Many people believed him.

Not everyone believed Lazar. There was no **proof** he worked at Area 51. People said he was lying. But others still thought Area 51 was hiding something. Soon there were many Area 51 stories. But what was the truth?

One story surrounding Area 51 was that the first manned moon landing in 1969 was fake. Some people think it was just filmed at a stage in Area 51.

CHAPTER 3

THE
Truth

For years the government said Area 51 was not real. That changed in 2013. The government shared some files. The files said what happened at Area 51. Now everyone knew the truth.

The government admitted Area 51 really did exist on August 16, 2013.

ENTERING AREA 51

The government did not hide spaceships. It had been making aircrafts. This was during the Cold War (1947–1991). The government was nervous about the Soviet Union. It did not want them to find out. So everything was kept secret.

The F-117 Nighthawk is one aircraft that has flown over Area 51.

THE COLD WAR

The Cold War was against the Soviet Union. It was not about battles. The countries were racing to make the best **technology**.

TESTING AIRCRAFT

The government tested aircraft at Area 51 for years. One was called the U-2. It flew higher than any other plane before. People would not have known what it was. That is why many thought they saw spaceships.

President Dwight D. Eisenhower wanted to test aircraft. He told the CIA to test the U-2. It was used for spying.

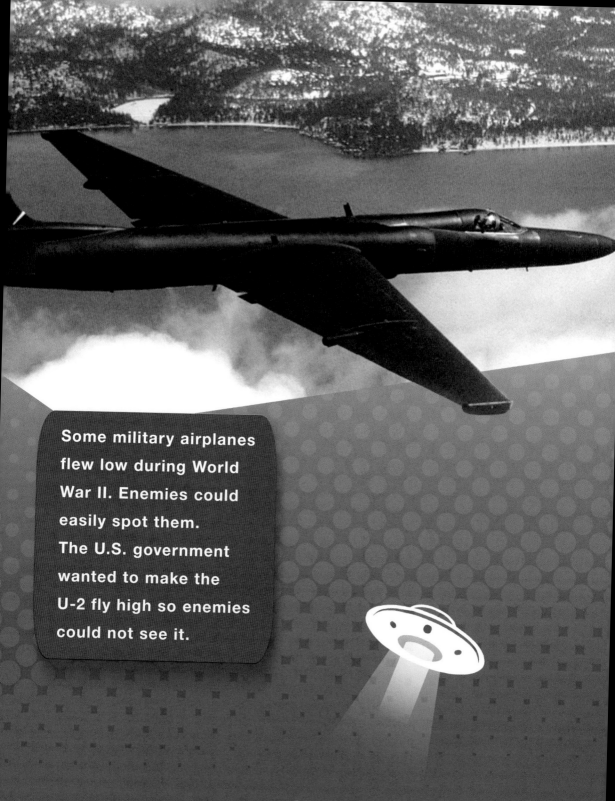

Some military airplanes flew low during World War II. Enemies could easily spot them. The U.S. government wanted to make the U-2 fly high so enemies could not see it.

Some of what people believed about Area 51 is true. The government did hide something there. It was an enemy plane. Scientists studied it. The government wanted to learn how it worked. The government wanted to make U.S. aircraft better.

Many tourist attractions are near Area 51, including the Alien Research Center gift shop.

Some people still think things are hidden at Area 51. Almost nobody knows what is going on there today. People try to get close to Area 51. They want to look for answers. The area is full of mystery.

GLOSSARY

alien
a creature not from Earth

proof
the facts that show something is true

technology
machines and things that are made using science

UFO
an unidentified flying object

TRIVIA

1. People ride on special government planes to get to work at Area 51.

2. The government calls Area 51 the Nevada Test and Training Range.

3. Area 51 is also next to the Nevada Test Site for nuclear machines. Area 51 is named for where it is marked on the map of the test site.

4. There is a hotel near Area 51 called the Little A'Le'Inn. People often stay there when they want to look for UFOs nearby.

ACTIVITY

WRITE ABOUT A TOP-SECRET PLACE

People came up with stories about Area 51 to guess what was happening there. Can you think of a place that is secret to you? What might happen there? Do you have proof of what happens there? If you can't think of a secret place, make up your own! Write a story about what happens in this secret place. Why is it kept secret? How do people find out what is happening there?

FURTHER RESOURCES

**Interested in learning more about aliens?
Check out these resources:**

Hunter, Nick. *Have Aliens Visited Earth?* Top Secret! Chicago, Illinois: Heinemann Raintree, 2016.

PBS: Search for Extraterrestrial Intelligence: Are We Alone? https://tpt.pbslearningmedia.org/resource/ess05.sci.ess.eiu.alone/search-for-extraterrestrial-intelligence-are-we-alone

Want to know more about Area 51 and other government secrets? Learn more with these resources:

Manzanero, Paula K. *Where Is Area 51?* Who HQ. New York: Penguin Workshop, 2018.

Reed, Ellis M. *Roswell.* Aliens. North Mankato, Minn.: Capstone Press, 2020.

INDEX